BREAK

Louise Rozett

BROADWAY PLAY PUBLISHING INC
New York
www.broadwayplaypublishing.com
info@broadwayplaypublishing.com

Cover image: Michael Rozett

First edition: April 2020
I S B N: 978-0-88145-868-8

Book design: Marie Donovan
Page make-up: Adobe InDesign
Typeface: Palatino

BREAK had a workshop/staged reading in 2004, when On the Leesh teamed up with the Naked Angels and took the play to New York Stage & Film. The cast was as follows:

OFFICER MARCO GENNARO .... Matthew Rashid
CAPTAIN JON EMMETT ....Frank Wood
DARLENE GENNARO .... Carey Peters
LISA EMMETT .... Anastasia Webb
ANNIE ....Jessica Arinella

Director ....Geoffrey Nauffts

BREAK received a five-performance Equity Showcase Production in 2011 at the New York International Fringe Festival, produced by Louise Rozett, Michael Rozett, and Tracy Middendorf. The cast was as follows:

OFFICER MARCO GENNARO .... Brian Patrick Murphy
CAPTAIN JON EMMETT ....John Finn
DARLENE GENNARO ....Jenny Dare Paulin
LISA EMMETT .... Liza J Bennett
ANNIE ....Gabrielle Sterbenz (Aimée)

Director .... Tracy Middendorf

ACKNOWLEDGMENTS

Special thanks to Jean and Ronald Rozett, Michael Rozett and Cara Lansden, Tracy Middendorf, David Mold, and Geoffrey Nauffts.

Thanks to the many people and organizations who helped develop BREAK over the last 18 years, including: Alicia Arinella, Jessica Arinella, Liza J Bennett, Jere Burns, Karl Bury, Jennifer Carta, Halle Charlton, William Charlton, David Dastmalchian, Julie Dretzin, Ensemble Studio Theatre Los Angeles, Mandy Fabian, John Finn, Carolyn Hoffman-Schneider, Yu-Han Huang, Patrick John Hurley, Spencer Kayden, Lindsey Kraft, Ericka Kreutz, Beth Lacke, Joseph Laney, Stacey Linden, Matt Lowe, Ann Maney, Brian Patrick Murphy, Naked Angels, Lethia Nall, New York International Fringe Festival, New York Stage & Film, Kathi O'Donohue, On the Leesh, Katie Page, Kirsten A Parker, Jenny Dare Paulin, Carey Peters, Tim Ransom, Matthew Rashid, Reverie Productions, Gabrielle Sterbenz, Anastasia Webb, Frank Wood, Colin D Young, Nicol Zanzarella, and all the Kickstarter Backers who contributed in 2011.

Thanks also to: Joseph Juliano, Julian Schlusberg, and the Hamden High School Theatre Department; and Dean Corrin, Jim Ostholthoff, and The Theatre School at DePaul University.

NOTE ON MUSIC

CHARACTERS & SETTING

OFFICER MARCO GENNARO, *male, late 20s, Brooklyn cop. As his wife describes him, a "hot-headed pain-in-the-ass."*

DARLENE GENNARO, *female, late 20s, MARCO's second wife. Tough as nails until she's not.*

CAPTAIN JON EMMETT, *male, early 50s, Staten Island fireman. A functioning alcoholic with a heart of gold.*

LISA EMMETT, *female, early to mid 20s, JON's daughter. Recovering addict, vulnerable with an edge.*

ANNIE, *female, 30s. A great listener whose good intentions occasionally get her in over her head.*

Ground Zero, New York City, December 23, 2001.
Also, a kitchen in Brooklyn, and a kitchen in Staten Island.

DEDICATION

After 9/11, I started volunteering in the respite tent at Ground Zero, serving food to the recovery workers. I met extraordinary people who were trying to accomplish a nearly impossible task. This play is an attempt to express gratitude to them for everything they did—often at great personal expense—to get New York City back on its feet.

For Lieutenant Jack Halaby, Engine 247

and

Firefighter Tommy Casatelli, Engine 247; Lieutenant
Bill D'Emic, Engine 254; Lieutenant George Farinacci;
Captain Jim Morgan;
Firefighter Steve Nuzzo, Ladder 156/Engine 276;
Chief James Riches; and
E S U Officers Danny Coan, Frank, and Murph

May your strength give us strength
May your faith give us faith
May your hope give us hope
May your love bring us love

Into the Fire, **Bruce Springsteen**

(Lights up on the recovery workers' dining room in the tent at Ground Zero, Sunday, December 23, 2001, 8 P M. Most of the pit crew is in the tent, waiting for the rain to let up. On the wall is a banner that reads, "Ground Zero Heroes: Thank You For All That You Do," with hundreds of signatures. The banner is half-heartedly decorated with cheap Christmas tinsel. A small, beat-up poinsettia, a stack of ratty looking newspapers, and a pile of cards written by school children all over the world to the Ground Zero heroes are on the table. MARCO GENNARO, a 29-year-old Brooklyn cop, sits by himself at a table for six with a tray of half-finished food in front of him. He's on his cell.)

GENNARO: Dar? …Dar… Ya gonna talk to me or am I just gonna talk to the answerin' machine all night…I know you're there…pick up…come on, Dar, pick up… if ya don't pick up I'll just keep callin' until the tape runs outs and then I'll call your cell til your voicemail is full…you know I'll do it, too…Ya wanna listen to me doin' this all night long? *(He listens. She doesn't pick up.)* Look, uh, I'm sorry about this mornin'…I shoulda told ya about all this but you gotta know I'm doin' it for *us*, not for *me*…Dar, I'm just gonna keep talking so you might as well pick up…. It's crappy down here tonight. Freezin' rain, just like the weatherman said. They found Robertson's kid, so that's good. At least he can get back to retirement now. He didn't take a single day off. Well, for his other kid's funeral, the fireman, he did…Dar, please pick up….

(CAPTAIN JON EMMETT, a Staten Island fireman, 51, appears. He's holding a tray and a New York Times, and

looking for somewhere to sit. He looks at GENNARO's *table, not wanting to sit there, but not having any other option. He gestures to* GENNARO. GENNARO *nods.* EMMETT *puts his tray down.* GENNARO *turns away from him.)*

GENNARO: Dar, just ten more days, that's all. We'll have another fight about it when I get home tomorrow morning, okay?

*(*EMMETT *laughs a little, and sits.* GENNARO *realizes* EMMETT *is listening, and pretends he's actually talking to Dar.)*

GENNARO: Okay, sure, yeah, I'll be home by nine. Kiss Mikey goodnight for me. See ya.

*(*GENNARO *puts his phone back in his pocket.* EMMETT *is busy with his food. His tray contains all the fixings for a huge sandwich. Throughout, he prepares the sandwich haphazardly, taking things off, putting other things on, cutting up vegetables. He never actually takes a bite.)*

EMMETT: Wife?

GENNARO: Yup.

EMMETT: Wants ya home?

GENNARO: Yeah, so she can kill me. Overtime means nothin' to a woman.

EMMETT: Shitty schedule, huh?

GENNARO: Oh yeah.

EMMETT: It's a little easier if no one's waitin' for ya at home.

GENNARO: I bet. *(He picks up a card from the pile. He reads and shakes his head. Indicating the card:)* Unbelievable, these kids.

EMMETT: What, those?

GENNARO: Yeah.

EMMETT: Ya got kids?

GENNARO: One. You?

EMMETT: I got boys in college. One of 'em is majoring in girls, the other one in beer

(Lights up stage right on EMMETT's daughter, LISA, 24, standing in his kitchen with a poinsettia, keys, and his New York Times. It's the same paper that he has with him.)

LISA: Anybody here? *(She looks at her watch, then sits down on the edge of a chair, still wearing her jacket. She looks around. She hasn't been here in two years.)*

GENNARO: You must be real proud.

EMMETT: Oh, yeah. If I'm lucky, they'll realize they should learn somethin' before they graduate. *(He starts to build his sandwich.)* We found one of your guys today.

GENNARO: Robertson.

EMMETT: Yeah. Ya know him?

GENNARO: No. How bad was he?

EMMETT: His badge was the only way.

GENNARO: Bullet in his head, right?

EMMETT: Yeah.

GENNARO: Yeah, I heard about that.

EMMETT: Trapped. Legs were crushed.

GENNARO: How long ya think he was like that before he used his gun?

EMMETT: No way to know.

GENNARO: Poor bastard.

EMMETT: Well, at least he had that option.

GENNARO: Option. He coulda been there for days. Must've taken some serious balls to make that decision.

EMMETT: Not when your only other choice is to die like that.

GENNARO: You think it's easy to put a bullet in your brain when you wanna live? *(He throws the card back onto the pile.)*

EMMETT: I could see what happened to the guy. He didn't wanna live.

(Lights up stage left on GENNARO's *wife,* DARLENE, *27, in a bathrobe, in their kitchen.)*

DARLENE: Ya want scrambled eggs? Marco? Ya hear me? Ya want scrambled eggs?

*(*DARLENE *turns on the radio and something like Bing Crosby's* I'll Be Home For Christmas *plays.)*

DARLENE: He can't hear me, scrambled eggs is what he's gettin'. He's lucky he's gettin' anythin' outta me this mornin'. *(She goes about the business of making eggs.)*

GENNARO: His old man see him?

EMMETT: He found him.

DARLENE: Do you hear me callin' you?

GENNARO: No.

EMMETT: Yup.

GENNARO: He did? He found him?

DARLENE: I'm makin' ya some eggs.

GENNARO: I didn't hear that. Jesus H. Don't that just beat all.

DARLENE: Marco!

GENNARO: I don't know what the fuck to make of that.

DARLENE: Is that what you want?!

GENNARO: *(To* DARLENE, *irritated by the interruption.)* Darlene, I have eggs every morning.

DARLENE: I just thought I'd ask ya. That's all. Just thought I'd ask ya.

GENNARO: He find the fireman kid, too?

EMMETT: No, I found him.

GENNARO: How bad was he?

EMMETT: This was in September, so you could still see the face. Back then, you could still see the—what, I don't know, the, the terror. On the face. The shock.

GENNARO: Did ya know him?

EMMETT: *(Nods)* I know his father.

(LISA reaches for a piece of a paper and a pen from the pile of stuff on the table. She starts to write a note, but doesn't get very far.)

GENNARO: The kid was alone?

EMMETT: The fireman was in the stairwell with a bunch of other guys. The cop today was alone.

GENNARO: Aw, nobody should have to go that way.

EMMETT: Must've been scared as hell.

GENNARO: It's pretty hard to scare a cop.

(EMMETT reaches for the salt and pepper.)

GENNARO: So, uh, how was Robertson, when he found the kid?

EMMETT: That was it for him.

GENNARO: Jesus. That old man was fuckin' runnin' himself into the ground, lookin' for that kid. Fifteen years on the force, twenty-three in the fire department, and he has to come out of retirement to dig his boys out of a pile of shit some fuckin' foreigners dumped on us 'cause our goddamn government was goddamn asleep at the wheel.

EMMETT: It's more complicated than that.

GENNARO: I don't think it is.

EMMETT: Sure it is.

GENNARO: How so?

EMMETT: Somebody's tryin' to tell us somethin'.

(GENNARO *scoffs.* EMMETT *reads his Times.* LISA *glances down at the paper and a headline gets her attention, distracting her from the work of writing the note.*)

GENNARO: (*Looking at* EMMETT *reading the Times, ignoring the pile of newspapers on the table. Pointedly:*) Where's today's *Post*?

(EMMETT *shrugs.* DARLENE *answers him as if he had just walked into the kitchen. She's irritated that he couldn't hear her before.*)

DARLENE: Outside on the steps, where it usually is in the mornin'.

(GENNARO *turns to her.*)

GENNARO: What, you don't read the paper anymore? (*He gets up and walks into his kitchen. He looks over her shoulder as she cooks.*) Hey, throw a little cheese in those eggs, would ya?

DARLENE: Absolutely not.

GENNARO: Come on.

DARLENE: Cholesterol.

(GENNARO *sighs.*)

DARLENE: You're welcome.

(GENNARO *exits, comes back with the Post, and sits at his kitchen table.*)

GENNARO: The weather's gonna be crappy tonight. Freezin' rain. It's not gonna be freezin', and it's not gonna rain. It's gonna be freezin' rain. Just what I need. Aw, Jesus. Look at this. The city wants to shut down Ground Zero for Christmas, but the firemen won't let 'em. Those guys. The same thing happened at Thanksgivin'. They won't take a goddamn break.

Which means the rest of us gotta work. I'm sure it'll be the same on New Year's. It ain't right. It just ain't right.

(DARLENE *snaps off the radio and looks at* GENNARO. *Without looking at her:)*

GENNARO: What.

DARLENE: Whaddya mean, "what".

GENNARO: I know you're lookin' at me. I can feel those Darlene Gennaro laser beams burnin' into my head. What.

DARLENE: Are ya gonna be home on time tonight?

GENNARO: There's no such thing as "on time" right now, Dar. I got my regular shifts, and the Pile shifts. That's the way it goes.

DARLENE: How can they still make ya work like that, after all this time?

GENNARO: It's only been a few months, Dar. Turned on the news lately? It's still a mess down there. Somebody's gotta deal with it.

DARLENE: Why you?

GENNARO: It's a crime scene. We gotta guard it.

DARLENE: For months and months? What are the rest of us supposed to do?

GENNARO: Wait it out. It ain't gonna be like this forever.

DARLENE: Well, it's a problem, Marco.

GENNARO: How is it a problem?

DARLENE: It's throwin' us off.

GENNARO: What do you want me to do, babe? We have to work down there right now. Nobody has a choice. It has to be protected twenty-four hours a day.

DARLENE: What about Danny? He had a choice.

GENNARO: Yeah, well, Danny was there that day.
They're not making those guys work the Pile. They
seen too much as it is. You want me to be one of them?
Danny spends half the day in bed at Ma's house. Some
days she can't even wake him up. He doesn't eat until
dinner. "Post-traumatic stress syndrome," whatever
the hell that is. *(He goes back to the paper.)* Mikey still
asleep?

DARLENE: Yeah.

GENNARO: How come?

DARLENE: I don't know, I guess he's tired.

GENNARO: He's a two-year-old. What's he got to be
tired about?

DARLENE: He played with Max yesterday.

GENNARO: Who's Max?

DARLENE: *(Annoyed that he can never remember this)* The
little boy across the street. They ran around Max's
playroom for a few hours.

GENNARO: They have a finished basement in that
house?

(DARLENE nods.)

GENNARO: They own that place?

DARLENE: Everybody on this block owns but us.

GENNARO: What are ya talkin' about? That's not true.
What about Sheila and Dave?

DARLENE: They bought last spring.

GENNARO: They did? Where'd they get the money?

DARLENE: How should I know? That's not somethin'
ya ask somebody when they tell ya they bought their
house.

GENNARO: How long they live there, the people across the street?

DARLENE: All I know is they're nice, and Mikey and Max like to run around together.

GENNARO: If they got a finished basement, they own it. That's what made Mikey so tired? Runnin' around a playroom with another two-year-old?

DARLENE: Max is a little older than him.

GENNARO: He shouldn't sleep so late. You should get him up.

DARLENE: You get him up. Ya haven't seen him or talked to him in two days.

GENNARO: Alls I'm sayin' is he's too young to be so tired.

DARLENE: You don't have to be a grown man with the weight of the world on your shoulders to be tired.

(LISA *looks up from the paper at* EMMETT. *She puts down the pen.*)

GENNARO: All right. What the hell is it that you are so pissed off about, Dar.

DARLENE: Are ya stupid? Or just deaf? What have we been talkin' about for the last five minutes?

GENNARO: You're mad at me 'cause I'm doin' my job? This is what I do. Ya can't say ya didn't know this was part of the deal. I was on the job three years when ya married me.

DARLENE: Yeah, well, who knew New York City was gonna fall down and you'd have to work twenty-four hours in a row every other day and never see your wife or your son. Yesterday he asked me if ya still lived here.

(DARLENE *cooks*, GENNARO *reads*.)

LISA: *(Stands, slowly, and holds up a key)* I still got a key.

(EMMETT stops fussing with his sandwich. He doesn't turn.)

EMMETT: Are ya okay?

LISA: I'm fine.

EMMETT: Ya sure?

LISA: Yeah, I'm sure. I'm fine.

EMMETT: What are ya doing here?

LISA: I figured ya wouldn't have any decorations up or anythin' so I brought ya this. Merry Christmas.

(EMMETT turns to look at LISA. She holds up the plant. He says nothing. She puts it on the table. He stands and crosses to a closet in the mud room area of the kitchen. He hangs his jacket up on a hook inside the door.)

LISA: I came to see ya.

(GENNARO looks up at DARLENE, watching her cook.)

EMMETT: *(Looking around the kitchen carefully)* How long ya been here?

LISA: Since seven. Workin'? At the firehouse?

EMMETT: The Pile.

LISA: Yeah?

EMMETT: I'm there for a month. I'm back tonight, so I gotta get some sleep.

(EMMETT crosses to the sink to wash his hands. Lisa isn't sure what to do.)

GENNARO: Dar. It ain't gonna be like this forever. They're gonna come up with some other way to do this thing.

DARLENE: My sister told me not to marry you. She said I'd be spendin' a lotta nights by myself. Now I know what she meant.

GENNARO: Yeah, well, in that case, your sister didn't choose too well herself.

DARLENE: Whaddya mean? Daryl's a good guy.

GENNARO: He works the night shift, Darlene. She spends *all* her nights alone.

DARLENE: Yeah, but they have all day together.

(LISA decides to sit back down. EMMETT is still at the sink, with his back to her, washing a plate, a knife, and a fork off the top of a big pile of dirty dishes.)

GENNARO: What, he never sleeps?

DARLENE: A few hours after he first gets home. Then they go food shoppin' together.

GENNARO: You hate food shoppin'.

DARLENE: No, I don't.

GENNARO: Since when do you like food shoppin'?

DARLENE: I've always liked food shoppin'. You just forgot.

GENNARO: You hate food shoppin'.

DARLENE: I must have been outta my mind, marryin' a cop. I don't know what the hell I was thinkin'.

GENNARO: Aw, yeah ya do. *(He sidles up to her, and puts his arms around her while she's cooking.)* You were thinkin', "Cops are hot. And that guy's gorgeous. I'm gonna marry me some hot, gorgeous cop," that's what you were thinkin'.

DARLENE: I must have been outta my mind.

GENNARO: You just couldn't resist my strikin' good looks, could ya, Dar.

DARLENE: What, ya think ya married an eighteen year-old? I was twenty-three when you married me. I knew better than to marry a hot-headed pain-in-the-ass from Brooklyn for his looks.

GENNARO: Aw, come on. Look at these eyes. And this jaw line. And what about all my big muscles.

DARLENE: When was the last time ya worked out?

(GENNARO *thinks for a moment, and can't remember.*)

GENNARO: It's not the muscles, huh? Oh. I know. Ya married me for my great intellect.

DARLENE: Yeah, that's it. You just keep tellin' yourself that.

GENNARO: Well, then, that only leaves one thing.

DARLENE: What.

GENNARO: My big, HUGE—

DARLENE: Shut up, Marco.

GENNARO: Yeah, baby, that's it. You married me for the hot sex.

DARLENE: Is the sex hot? I really can't remember, it's been so long.

(DARLENE *turns to face* GENNARO, *his arms still around her.*)

DARLENE: Remind me.

(DARLENE *and* GENNARO *look at each other, and then he releases her and goes back to the table.*)

GENNARO: Those eggs ready? I gotta go.

(DARLENE *scrapes the eggs onto a plate and drops the plate in front of* GENNARO, *but she doesn't put down the fork. He looks happily at the eggs, and then up at her, and then at the fork. She sits. As he reaches for the fork and she pulls it away,* EMMETT, *fork in hand, takes a dishtowel and starts to dry the fork, and then the other washed items.*)

DARLENE: The last two months, ya come home and ya look half dead. I ask ya to go check on your son, ya say ya don't wanna wake him up. We get into bed, and you're asleep before I can tell you the cute or smart thing Mikey said or did that day. And forget about makin' love. I can't remember the last time that happened. It wasn't that long ago, Marco, that I had to fight you off. At least twice a day. Now ya barely look at me in the bedroom. You didn't even notice what I was wearin' last night when you finally came to bed— and trust me, the old you woulda noticed this. You're not interested and I wanna know why.

(GENNARO *looks away first.* EMMETT *still has his back to Lisa.*)

LISA: Ya want me to go?

EMMETT: Ya need somethin'?

LISA: Nope.

EMMETT: I didn't know ya still had a key.

LISA: I was surprised it still worked. Sorry. I didn't, I didn't mean to…

(EMMETT *lets* LISA *trail off, offering no acceptance of her apology.*)

EMMETT: Okay. Well. I'm gonna eat something and go to bed.

LISA: Don't they feed ya down there?

EMMETT: I ain't really hungry 'til I get home.

LISA: Hard work?

EMMETT: It's fine.

(EMMETT *puts the dried plate, knife, and fork on the counter. He opens the fridge, which contains only a loaf of bread, some butter, and a few tomatoes. He takes them out and puts a piece of bread from the loaf in the toaster.*)

LISA: No, I'm not hungry. Thanks for askin'.

(EMMETT *ignores this, carefully slicing a tomato.* GENNARO *puts his hand out and reaches for the fork.*)

GENNARO: My eggs are getting' cold and I'm gonna be late for work.

DARLENE: Tell me why right now or you're gonna be wearin' your eggs, Officer Gennaro.

GENNARO: Dar. I'm workin' twenty-four hour shifts with no sleep. And it ain't exactly desk work. I'm just tired. And right now, I'm really hungry. Can I have the fork? Please? Pretty, pretty, please, Pretty Darlene?

DARLENE: Don't call me pretty just 'cause you want somethin'.

GENNARO: Sorry, babe. You're right. You're not pretty. You're beautiful.

DARLENE: I'm gonna ask ya this once, Marco, that's all. So you better listen carefully. Are you ready? Is. There. Some. One. Else.

GENNARO: Darlene. What the hell is wrong with you? You're insane, ya know that? Jesus Christ.

DARLENE: Stop takin' the Lord's name in vain.

GENNARO: Gimme the fork.

DARLENE: Answer the question!

(GENNARO *gets a fork from the drawer. He angrily eats his eggs in about three bites. He gets up to go. The look on* DARLENE'S *face stops him. After a moment, he sits back down.*)

GENNARO: Okay, Screwball, listen to me. First of all, I don't want anybody else. That's why I married *you.* Second of all, I would never have the guts to cheat on you because you'd kick my ass. And third of all, when would I have the time? If I'm not on duty, I'm downtown, bustin' my ass. It's not exactly a party down there. At least not for the cops.

(EMMETT *takes his piece of toast out of the toaster and puts it on the plate. He puts a slice of tomato on it.*)

DARLENE: Ya never say anythin' about what ya do down there.

GENNARO: Ya never ask.

DARLENE: I'm askin' now.

GENNARO: I tell tourists to stop crowdin' the barricades. I check I Ds. I try to stop 'em from takin' pictures but they don't listen. I give 'em directions to Century 21 because they still want to see it even after I tell 'em it's closed. That's it.

DARLENE: Ya don't say what ya see. Ya don't tell me any of the bad stuff.

GENNARO: Why do ya wanna know that, Darlene? It's bad enough I gotta carry that around with me, why do you want to?

DARLENE: Why do you gotta carry that stuff around by yourself? What am I here for?

GENNARO: To cook my breakfast and take care of my son.

(*This really pisses* DARLENE *off.*)

GENNARO: I'm kiddin'! Dar, I'm kiddin'. That was a joke.

DARLENE: You always gotta make a joke when we're talkin' about somethin' real.

GENNARO: No, I don't.

DARLENE: Yeah, ya do. That's how ya cope.

GENNARO: Aw, here we go again with all that crap. Stop watchin' Oprah or I'm getting' a divorce.

DARLENE: You go ahead and call it whatever you want, Marco. It's the truth, that's all I know.

GENNARO: What's the real problem here, Dar?

DARLENE: How the hell am I gonna get pregnant again if you're never here?

GENNARO: The mailman.

DARLENE: Don't tempt me, Marco.

GENNARO: Oh yeah, I'm really worried about you and the mailman. The guy's like ninety.

DARLENE: Yeah, well, I see him a lot more often than I see you.

GENNARO: You see him once a day for two minutes.

DARLENE: I see you once a day for five minutes. What's the difference? Two minutes and five minutes are the same thing, as far as a woman is concerned. So? How come I'm not pregnant?

GENNARO: I don't know, maybe you oughta see a doctor about that.

DARLENE: Again with that stupid joke thing.

GENNARO: Yeah, yeah, yeah.

(DARLENE *picks up the plate and the pan and tosses them into the sink, making a racket. She starts to wash. He stands there watching her.* EMMETT *takes a bite of his tomato toast.*)

EMMETT: What's the note say?

LISA: What?

EMMETT: The note you were writing. On the table.

LISA: Oh. Nothin'.

EMMETT: You wrote somethin'.

(LISA *picks it up.*)

LISA: "Hi, I…"

EMMETT: That's it?

LISA: Yeah.

EMMETT: What was the rest of it gonna say?

LISA: I don't know. Maybe, um, "How are you? I am fine. I moved to a new place—"

EMMETT: Ya livin' with friends or somethin'?

LISA: Yeah.

EMMETT: Dominic?

LISA: Jesus, no. I got rid of him a long time ago.

EMMETT: Good. Do I know 'em? The friends you're livin' with?

LISA: They're not from here.

EMMETT: Whaddya mean, they're not from here? Where they from? Mars or somethin'?

LISA: I just meant they're not from Staten Island.

EMMETT: Well where're they from?

LISA: Manhattan.

EMMETT: Nobody's from Manhattan.

LISA: That's where they live. That's where I live now.

EMMETT: Ya like it?

LISA: Yeah. A lot.

EMMETT: How'd ya meet 'em?

LISA: Friend of a friend. Worked out great.

EMMETT: How ya payin' for that?

(LISA *doesn't answer* EMMETT. GENNARO *crosses to his chair, turns it to face* DARLENE, *sits, and waits.*)

EMMETT: So what are ya doin' in my kitchen?

LISA: I didn't know I wasn't allowed to visit.

EMMETT: Well, usually a person visits another person when that person is home. Or a person calls first.

LISA: I thought I'd just come by.

EMMETT: What do ya need?

LISA: Why do ya think I need somethin'?

EMMETT: I can't think of any other reason for ya to come see me.

LISA: It's not possible that I just wanted to see ya?

EMMETT: Anything's possible, Lisa.

LISA: I didn't take anythin'.

EMMETT: I didn't say ya did.

LISA: I just wanted to see ya.

(EMMETT *stops what he's doing.*)

EMMETT: Why?

LISA: I been thinkin' about ya.

EMMETT: Oh yeah?

LISA: Yeah. A lot. I called Bobby.

EMMETT: He told me.

LISA: Doesn't that count?

EMMETT: Whaddya mean, "count"? I don't know what that means.

LISA: Ya thought I wasn't worried about ya?

EMMETT: I wasn't really thinkin' about you at all.

(EMMETT *puts a second piece of toast in the toaster.* LISA *is clearly uncomfortable. She waits for a response, and then starts to examine the poinsettia.* DARLENE *stops cleaning up and turns to* GENNARO.)

DARLENE: Ya know what I think?

GENNARO: Would I still be here if I knew the answer to that question? I never know what you think, Darlene. You're a freakin' mystery to me.

DARLENE: I think, even though ya said, when we got married, that we were gonna have lots of babies, I think ya changed your mind and you're too chicken-shit to tell me.

GENNARO: Darlene, we can't afford another kid. I'm barely makin' it work as it is. I can't even buy the Christmas presents I wanna buy this year. I got the alimony until Sherri marries that Staten Island jerk-off. I gotta help out my folks as much as I can—I'm all they got right now—who knows if Danny's ever gonna go back to the force. And I got you and Mikey here at home. You're not workin' anymore—

DARLENE: You said that was okay with you.

GENNARO: It is okay with me, but on one salary, we can't have another kid. It's impossible.

DARLENE: You're lyin'.

GENNARO: What did you say to me?

DARLENE: I said, you're lyin'. That's not the real reason. We sat down and figured out our money after we had Mikey and we were fine. We haven't gone on a vacation in two years. We don't go out to eat. We don't buy anything. Last Christmas you wanted to get us that D V D player and a wide-screen T V—you been talking about that forever—but you didn't. Why? Because we're savin' money. I always know when you're lyin' and you know I always know when you're lyin', so do not bullshit me, Marco.

GENNARO: I'm not bullshitting ya!

(EMMETT *turns to look at* LISA, *who is picking the less-than-perfect leaves off the poinsettia.*)

DARLENE: Oh yeah ya are. I can see it in your eyes. You're the world's worst liar. Why don't you want another baby?

(GENNARO *doesn't say anything.*)

DARLENE: We need to go talk to Father O'Neill.

GENNARO: No! No way. I'm not goin' to a priest. I'm sick of priests.

DARLENE: *(Surprised by his vehemence)* Marco, come on.

GENNARO: It's the truth, Dar. I'm done with 'em.

DARLENE: Whaddya mean, you're done with priests? What'd they ever do to you?

GENNARO: "God works in mysterious ways," "God has his reasons," "We can never know God's plan." I can't deal with that crap anymore. I'm tired of listenin' to 'em.

DARLENE: Since when?

GENNARO: They're always comin' around now, tryin' to get us to talk.

DARLENE: They're tryin' to help.

GENNARO: I don't need their help. Let 'em go help somebody else.

DARLENE: Is that why ya won't go to church anymore?

GENNARO: What about all those fuckin' funerals? That's not church?

DARLENE: Sorry, babe. I'm sorry. I just meant, I meant that ya haven't been to church with us. That's all.

GENNARO: I had enough church in the last three months to last me the rest of my life, so don't tell me I haven't been to goddamn church. And I'm not done yet. There's more funerals where those came from. Probably enough to last me a whole 'nother year.

Maybe you should come with me sometime. Then you'll see why I'm sick of the whole thing.

DARLENE: I'd go with ya if ya ask me.

GENNARO: I gotta ask? You know, sometimes I think you don't get it. You don't get what happened. What's still happenin'. I don't care, Dar. I don't care about Father O'Neill or church or any of that shit. I don't even believe in God right now.

DARLENE: Marco!

GENNARO: Hey, ya wanted the truth? There it is. That's the truth.

(GENNARO *takes the* Post *and goes back to the table in the recovery tent.* DARLENE *watches him go, and then goes back to the sink to finish cleaning up.* EMMETT *takes his second piece of toast out of the toaster and prepares it.)*

LISA: I wanted to call ya, but ya never really enjoyed hearin' from me.

EMMETT: It's been a lotta bad news from you.

LISA: I figured ya wouldn't wanna deal with me. With so much goin' on. But I was worried.

EMMETT: I don't think ya came by just to check on me.

LISA: It's been more than two years. People change.

EMMETT: People don't change.

LISA: Of course they do.

EMMETT: Do ya still lie?

LISA: I just wanted to make sure ya were okay.

(EMMETT *bites into his second piece of toast standing up, leaning against the counter.)*

LISA: I saw ya on T V the other night and ya looked like shit and I got, I got worried.

EMMETT: Because of the Trade Center?

LISA: No, because of your haircut. Yeah, because of the Trade Center.

EMMETT: It happened months ago. You're worried now?

LISA: I been worried since it happened. That lady from Fox looked like she was buggin' ya.

EMMETT: Those reporters'll suck the blood out of ya if ya ain't careful.

LISA: She asked stupid questions.

EMMETT: She asked the same questions everyone's askin' firemen right now.

LISA: They're stupid.

EMMETT: You're right.

LISA: Ya did a good job.

EMMETT: I don't remember what I said.

LISA: She asked how many guys ya knew. You said about a hundred. Is that true? Dad?

(EMMETT *doesn't answer.* GENNARO *picks up a card off the pile.*)

LISA: That's a lot of people.

EMMETT: There's guys out there who lost more than that. Guys who lost family.

LISA: I thought those guys *were* your family.

EMMETT: It's different.

LISA: I don't see how. Whaddya do on the pile?

(EMMETT *puts down the rest of his toast and wipes his hands and mouth with a napkin. Finally:*)

EMMETT: Search for human remains. We wait for a crane to dump a pile of debris, and we comb through it until we find a piece of a body. If it's small, we bag it. If it's big, we get the E M Ts.

LISA: Why do you have to pick through everythin'?

EMMETT: We gotta check everythin' before it goes to the dump. It gets checked there again. We're lookin' for personal items, anythin' we can return to the families. We're also lookin' for—

LISA: No, I mean why do you YOU have to pick through everythin'? Why the fire department?

EMMETT: Why wouldn't it be us?

LISA: I don't know. It just doesn't seem like it should be your job.

(A pissed off DARLENE loudly puts a dried plate away.)

EMMETT: Who else is gonna do it?

LISA: Somebody who's actually trained to look for things like human remains.

EMMETT: Who the hell would that be?

LISA: I don't know, but it shouldn't be you guys.

EMMETT: Sure it should.

LISA: Why?

EMMETT: We're alive. We might as well make ourselves useful.

(DARLENE loudly puts the dried pan away.)

LISA: Have ya seen anyone?

EMMETT: Whaddya mean?

LISA: Have ya found anyone ya know?

(EMMETT turns, takes the plate with toast and tomato on it, and dumps the rest in the very full trashcan. DARLENE finishes putting the dishes away and exits.)

GENNARO: Can ya believe the letters from these kids? Some of 'em got pictures, pictures of their entire classes, with all these little things written on 'em. Incredible.

(EMMETT *puts the plate and knife back on top of the pile in the sink.*)

EMMETT: They're nice, aren't they?

GENNARO: Some are a little weird, I gotta say.

EMMETT: The ones with the drawings?

(GENNARO *holds out a card and* EMMETT *crosses to the table and sits, looking at it.* LISA *watches him go, then purposefully takes her coat off and hangs it in the closet.*)

GENNARO: The religious ones. "God loves you," "God will save you," "God protects you." It's weird for little kids to say that stuff.

EMMETT: Religion seems to be makin' a comeback.

GENNARO: Naw, that shit never went away.

(EMMETT *laughs.* GENNARO *continues looking at cards.* LISA *comes back into the kitchen, takes a moment, and then picks up the poinsettia. She exits into the living room to find a good place for it.*)

EMMETT: Catholic school?

GENNARO: All twelve years.

EMMETT: Me, too.

GENNARO: Twelve years too many, if ya ask me.

EMMETT: Twelve years is a lotta school.

GENNARO: 'Specially Catholic school. Damn nuns and priests. They'll screw up your head good. Better off without 'em.

EMMETT: Strayed from the flock, huh?

GENNARO: I don't think there ever was a flock, not to mention a fuckin' shepherd. (*Indicating the card he's looking at.*) I find this shit creepy. Some little kid in Iowa wrote this: "Dear Fireman, I want to say thank you to you for all you do at Ground Zero. We are all thinking about you all the time. God is watching you and looking out for you, and He will take all your lost friends and family to the much better place. So don't worry." What is that? That kid has no idea what he's sayin'. He's just sayin' what he thinks he supposed to say.

EMMETT: He's just tryin' to thank us.

GENNARO: Yeah, yeah, sure, but who fed the kid that crap?

EMMETT: Someone who didn't think it was crap.

GENNARO: It is crap.

EMMETT: I'm sorry ya feel that way.

GENNARO: Don't be. It works out just fine for me.

EMMETT: Are you always so pissed off?

GENNARO: Hey, you sat here, buddy.

EMMETT: Nowhere else to sit. You're takin' up a whole table for six.

GENNARO: Nowhere else to sit.

EMMETT: Ya ever sat with a fireman down here before?

GENNARO: Why would I sit with someone I don't know?

EMMETT: You don't know any firemen?

GENNARO: Nope. No point in minglin'.

EMMETT: Doesn't seem to be, no. Unless there's nowhere else to sit.

GENNARO: Where're your guys? Why ain't you sittin' with them?

EMMETT: They don't always come in here. Some work out at that gym, some go to the church.

GENNARO: Yeah, and some go to the Lodge.

EMMETT: If they do, I don't know about it.

GENNARO: Yeah, I'm sure you don't.

EMMETT: I don't. But I can understand how a man might need a drink after a few hours on the pile.

GENNARO: What if he's drivin' a crane or a truck? You still think it's okay if he needs a drink?

EMMETT: I'm not sayin' it's okay to drink on the job. I'm sayin' I can understand how a man would want to. I don't touch it anymore, but that don't mean I don't think about it out there.

(A young woman in a blue volunteer apron approaches.)

ANNIE: *(Indicating GENNARO's tray.)* Can I take that for you?

GENNARO: *(The expert flirt instantly turns on the charm.)* Naw, that's all right, sweetheart, I can bus my own tray.

ANNIE: If you don't let me take your tray, I'll have to wander around, looking for someone who will. And if I don't find anyone, I'll have to take out the garbage. So let me take your tray. It's my job.

GENNARO: That's okay, hon. I'll take care of it.

ANNIE: *(To EMMETT)* Will you tell him to let me take his tray?

EMMETT: *(Kindly)* It doesn't feel right to have people waitin' on us.

(LISA enters. She crosses to the counter to check on the plants there, which are nearly dead. She moves some of the dirty dishes aside in order to water them. She plucks off the dead leaves, making a pile on the counter.)

ANNIE: It's really the least we can do.

(ANNIE reaches for GENNARO's tray. He puts his hand on it.)

GENNARO: *(Joking with her)* I'm not done yet.

ANNIE: Your plates are piled up, your utensils are in the middle, you finished your soda—I'd say you're done. Although it doesn't look like you've had dessert. Have you had the pudding? That bakery up on Church made it, and it's incredible.

EMMETT: I haven't tried the pudding yet.

ANNIE: Oh, you have to try the pudding. Now come on, Officer, let me take your tray and I'll get you both some pudding.

GENNARO: Instead of worryin' about my tray, why don't ya sit down and talk to us for a while.

(DARLENE enters with a basket of laundry. She sets it on the kitchen table and starts folding.)

ANNIE: It's too busy for me to take a break. I'll get fired.

GENNARO: How do you get fired from a volunteer job?

ANNIE: They tell you not to come back.

GENNARO: Aw, come on, I been watchin' ya since I got here, and ya haven't sat down once. You're movin' faster than any of the others. Ya make 'em look like they're standin' still. I bet ya haven't had dinner yet. Go get yourself some dinner and come back and sit down.

ANNIE: To be honest with you, they don't really like us sitting with the workers. Well, that's not exactly true. They don't really like some of us sitting with the workers.

EMMETT: You're kidding.

GENNARO: Really?

ANNIE: Apparently there have been some incidents. Or rumors of incidents.

EMMETT: Like what? People getting to know each other?

ANNIE: People getting to know each other too well.

GENNARO: What's "too well"?

ANNIE: In the showers. But it's just a rumor. And supposedly it only happened once.

GENNARO: No shit. Was it a fireman?

ANNIE: I don't know. But it's made life a lot tougher for the rest of us, that's for sure.

GENNARO: Aw, come on, I think you know. I'm guessin' fireman. Am I right? Those fireman, I tell ya—

ANNIE: I really don't know. But I shouldn't sit. I can already feel the shift supervisor staring at the back of my head.

EMMETT: That's too bad.

ANNIE: It's ridiculous. It makes me feel like a thirteen-year-old at a school dance.

GENNARO: Part of your job is to talk to us, right? To chat us up and distract us from what we're doin' out there?

ANNIE: Depends on who you ask. We're not supposed to "fraternize." That's for the mental health workers.

GENNARO: Aw, Jesus, those people drive me nuts. Ya can't even sit by yourself down here. They come over and start askin' ya about your "feelings." They're even worse than the priests.

EMMETT: That's their job. They're here to make sure we don't lose it on account of everything we're doin' and seein'.

(LISA *takes the pile of dead leaves over to the trashcan. There's no room. She puts the leaves back down on the counter and looks for a trash bag under the sink.*)

ANNIE: I'm sure you've seen some awful things.

EMMETT: *(Matter-of-factly)* I'll never forget some of the stuff I seen down here.

GENNARO: Aw, poor firemen.

EMMETT: *(Restraining himself a bit)* We're *on* the Pile. Where are you? Standin' up above, watching. What do you actually see? What do you have to touch?

GENNARO: I seen enough.

EMMETT: Yeah? Where? Where do you see anything?

GENNARO: I was in the Medical Examiner's office and the morgue for a month. I saw a fuckin' guy impaled on his own laptop. Don't tell me I didn't see anythin'. *(To* ANNIE:*)* Sorry. You didn't need to hear that.

ANNIE: It's okay.

*(*LISA *finds a trash bag and puts the dead leaves in it. She proceeds to change the bag in the can.)*

GENNARO: Go on. Go get yourself some food. It's been a hell of a day, and you'd be doin' us a favor. If anyone gives you a hard time, we'll talk to 'em for ya. Come on, we could use a pretty distraction.

(This embarrasses ANNIE, *but she looks around to see if anyone has noticed that she's been in one place too long.* DARLENE *stops folding. She takes a shirt off the pile, considers it, and checks the pockets. She doesn't find anything. She refolds it.)*

ANNIE: Well, I guess if I have food in front of me, it'll be okay. You guys need anything?

GENNARO: No, no, we're good.

ANNIE: No pudding?

EMMETT/GENNARO: *(Ad lib)* No! No way! / No pudding! / I'm eatin' too much down here as it is. / I'm gainin' weight.

ANNIE: (*Laughing at their outburst*) All right, I'll be back.

(ANNIE *exits.* GENNARO *watches her go, turning his head sideways for more of a view.*)

GENNARO: Nice, right? Very nice.

EMMETT: (*Ignoring his meaning, starting to fix his sandwich again*) All these people down here are nice.

GENNARO: Some of 'em are nicer than others.

(DARLENE *searches through the pile for a pair of pants. She checks the pockets. Nothing. She refolds. She goes back to folding the rest of the laundry.*)

EMMETT: Some of 'em came from Canada and California, one guy the other day was from Alaska. I can't believe these people gave up their holidays to come here. Gives ya hope.

(LISA *takes the trash out the backdoor.*)

GENNARO: For what?

EMMETT: The future. Human beings.

GENNARO: You're outta your head. Who do you think got us into this shit in the first place?

EMMETT: It wasn't these people.

GENNARO: Might as well be. Coulda been. Human beings.

EMMETT: Good and bad in everybody. Sometimes one wins out over the other.

GENNARO: Jesus, what are ya, a priest or somethin'? You a minister? A reverend? What's the story with you? Ya on a mission? Can't I just sit here in peace and not have to think about any of this?

(EMMETT *holds his hand up in apology.*)

EMMETT: Sorry. I didn't mean to proselytize.

GENNARO: (*Irritated that he doesn't know the word*) What?

EMMETT: I didn't mean to sound like a priest.

GENNARO: Not everybody believes what you believe.

EMMETT: I know that.

GENNARO: What you believe isn't the only thing to believe.

EMMETT: I know that, too.

GENNARO: No, ya know what? I don't think you do.

EMMETT: Easy there, buddy. We're just having a conversation.

GENNARO: Not anymore, we're not.

EMMETT: How old are you?

GENNARO: Why?

EMMETT: You're about thirty?

GENNARO: Next month. Why?

EMMETT: You're too young to be so mad.

(ANNIE *returns with a wrapped sandwich, a bottle of water, and one brownie. She sits.*)

ANNIE: I'm very sorry to report that the pudding is long gone, as usual. But I did manage to get one of the best brownies in the greater Metropolitan area. Don't panic, I just got one for the table. If we split it three ways, we'll all be okay, calorie-wise.

(*Neither* EMMETT *or* GENNARO *says anything. She unwraps her sandwich, takes a bite, and addresses* GENNARO.)

ANNIE: So how is it out there today? Cold and wet?

(ANNIE *is looking at* GENNARO, *who doesn't say anything.* EMMETT *steps in.*)

EMMETT: Yeah, but it could be a lot worse. We been lucky so far, thank god.

GENNARO: God has nothin' to do with it. It's just luck. That's all.

(There's an uncomfortable silence.)

GENNARO: So what's your name, volunteer lady?

(DARLENE looks at GENNARO.)

ANNIE: Anne. Well, Annie, really. Everybody calls me Annie.

GENNARO: I like that name. It's cute. Like the little girl with the red hair and the dog.

(DARLENE puts the folded laundry in the basket and exits with it.)

ANNIE: I even had a dog who looked like hers. His name wasn't Sandy though.

GENNARO: What was it?

ANNIE: Bob.

EMMETT: You had a dog named Bob?

ANNIE: I named him after my father.

GENNARO: Your father was okay livin' in a house with a dog who had his name?

ANNIE: Most people called my dad Robert, so there was rarely any kind of confusion.

EMMETT: Where ya from?

ANNIE: Upper west side.

EMMETT: You're a local, huh?

GENNARO: Everybody else I've met is from Alabama, Florida, Mississippi….

ANNIE: Amazing, isn't it?

EMMETT: What do you do when you're not here?

ANNIE: I'm a teacher. Fourth grade.

EMMETT: Well it's nice of ya to volunteer your time.

(LISA *comes back in. She goes to the sink to wash her hands.*)

ANNIE: I'd help out there if they'd let me. But I think I'd be a bit of a liability.

EMMETT: There are plenty of us diggin'. It's good for us to have nice people in here to talk to. It helps.

(GENNARO *rolls his eyes and sighs loudly.*)

ANNIE: It does?

EMMETT: 'Course it does.

ANNIE: I'm glad. I wish our supervisors believed that.

GENNARO: Annie, I got a question for ya.

EMMETT: Whatever it is, ya don't have to answer it.

GENNARO: Annie, ya believe in God?

EMMETT: Especially that.

GENNARO: Why not? Too personal? I'm sorry, Annie, is that a personal question?

ANNIE: It is, but I'll answer it. As long as you don't tell anybody— (*Indicating the volunteer apron*) I'm not supposed to talk religion or politics while I'm wearing this.

EMMETT: Ya don't have to.

GENNARO: Let her answer.

ANNIE: It's not a very clear answer.

GENNARO: What's the answer?

ANNIE: Sometimes. Maybe. I usually fluctuate between atheism and agnosticism several times during the course of a day.

(EMMETT *laughs.* LISA *notices a pile of memos on the counter while she's drying her hands. She picks one up and reads.*)

ANNIE: I wasn't brought up in a particularly God-heavy household.

EMMETT: How you're brought up has a lot to do with it.

GENNARO: I was brought up Catholic. I went through twelve years of Catholic school. I had God drilled into my head day in and day out. Wouldn't ya think I'd believe in God?

ANNIE: You don't?

GENNARO: Nope.

ANNIE: Why not?

GENNARO: You been out there? You seen that pile?

ANNIE: Not the way you have.

GENNARO: I don't know how anyone who has seen it and smelled it, and seen what's in it, could still think there's a God who gives two shits about the world.

EMMETT: What about in here? What's out there is more important than what's in here?

GENNARO: What's in here? Free food? Coffee? Pretty girls? *(To ANNIE, genuinely)* No offense.

ANNIE: None taken.

EMMETT: Good people. Nice people. People lookin' out for each other.

GENNARO: It's just food and a place to get outta the cold.

EMMETT: Sometimes that's all you need.

GENNARO: Aw, Jesus, come on.

EMMETT: If ya want to see it, ya will. If ya don't, ya won't.

GENNARO: That's a good argument to prove God's existence.

EMMETT: I'm not tryin' to prove nothin'.

GENNARO: Yeah ya are.

EMMETT: I'm startin' to find you offensive.

GENNARO: I found you offensive a long time ago.

EMMETT: It's Christmas time. Lighten up.

GENNARO: Why? I gotta have faith because it's almost December 25th? Is somebody gonna strike me down? Are you worried about my wellbeing? Isn't that sweet.

EMMETT: As a fellow human being, yes. As an individual, no.

ANNIE: How did we get on this topic?

GENNARO: Long story.

ANNIE: Are you guys friends?

EMMETT/GENNARO: No.

ANNIE: Do you know each other?

EMMETT/GENNARO: No.

ANNIE: You just met?

EMMETT: Yeah.

ANNIE: And this is your first conversation?

EMMETT: Uh-huh.

ANNIE: That's a hell of a way to get to know each other.

(DARLENE *enters and leans against the counter, watching* GENNARO.)

GENNARO: We ain't tryin' to get to know each other. We're tryin' to tolerate each other because there's nowhere else to sit, and it ain't workin' out so well. *(He feels the beginnings of a migraine.)* But don't you worry about it, hon. This ain't your problem.

DARLENE: Marco.

(ANNIE *eats her sandwich.* EMMETT *takes his apart and starts over.* LISA *turns the page of the memo she's reading.* DARLENE *makes a peace offering.*)

DARLENE: You getting' one of those headaches?

GENNARO: No.

DARLENE: I'm sorry I bugged ya about church.

GENNARO: *(Still pissed off.)* It's okay.

DARLENE: C'mere.

(GENNARO *reluctantly crosses into the kitchen.* DARLENE *puts her arms around him.*)

DARLENE: You understand why I want another baby, don't ya?

(GENNARO *doesn't answer.*)

DARLENE: Because of you, Marco. Because of us. We make good kids. Mikey's the sweetest, greatest kid in the world. And the world needs all the good people it can get.

GENNARO: The world won't even be here by the time he's old enough to do anything about anything.

DARLENE: Don't say that, babe.

GENNARO: It's true.

DARLENE: Even if it is true, we can't live like that. We gotta live like it's gonna go on forever. Otherwise we won't be able to get outta bed in the mornin'.

(GENNARO *shakes his head.*)

DARLENE: What?

GENNARO: Nothin'.

DARLENE: Just tell me what you're thinkin'. For once in your life, don't make me beg. Just say it.

GENNARO: I don't tell ya about workin' down there because you don't wanna hear it. I can see it in your face. And ya just said it. Ya wanna go on like nothin' happened.

DARLENE: That's not what I said.

GENNARO: If you were really thinkin' about what happened, you wouldn't want another baby. Look at what's goin' on. People from all over the world are comin' here to kill us. They're willin' to die to kill us. New York City is one big ground zero for the next attack. My own brother, he's been on the job since he was eighteen years old, he may never be a cop again because of what he saw that day. I can't protect anybody from that shit, least of all you. Or Mikey. I can't even protect my own son.

DARLENE: Marco, you're not a superhero. You're a cop. Mikey still wants ya to read to him whether you can save the world or not.

GENNARO: If I can't protect you and Mikey, I can't do my fuckin' job, Dar. And if I can't do my fuckin' job, what am I? It's too big now. If there is a God up there, he's not payin' attention or he doesn't care.

DARLENE: So we gotta live like we're dead because somethin' bad happened?

GENNARO: There it is. That's what I mean. You call it "somethin' bad."

DARLENE: You can't even say that much. You just keep sayin' "because of what happened."

GENNARO: Yeah, but I'm in it. I see it every day. You won't even touch the newspaper anymore—you can go through a whole day without even thinkin' about it.

DARLENE: I worry about you bein' down there every minute of every day, seein' the bodies, breathin' the air, dealin' with the crazy people who think they're at some kinda holy site. Don't think for a second that I don't worry or think about what you're goin' through.

So life is dangerous and scary. That's no reason not to have a family.

GENNARO: We already have a family.

DARLENE: Not the family we planned.

GENNARO: Our savings—all those stocks and crap— they're cut in half right now. We don't own anything worth owning. Even our fuckin' cars are leased. Ya want me to be one of those guys with two jobs who sees his wife and kid once a week? Ya want me to work more extra shifts? Or should I just start throwin' our money away on lottery tickets? I don't sleep well at night as it is, Dar—the last thing I need is another kid. What? Why you lookin' at me like that?

DARLENE: More extra shifts?

GENNARO: I just meant extra shifts. You're already complaining about how I'm never here, ya want me out more nights of the week?

DARLENE: So why'd ya say "more"?

GENNARO: I don't know. I didn't mean it like that. That's not what I meant.

DARLENE: So what did ya mean?

GENNARO: When did you get so suspicious of me? When did that happen?

DARLENE: When you stopped comin' home.

GENNARO: Alls I meant was I could pick up overtime right now. There's a lot of people who don't wanna work down there—I could work as much as I want. They're not payin' attention to who's doin' what because they need the manpower. The money's great. That's all.

(Pause. DARLENE *is staring at* GENNARO.*)*

DARLENE: You been workin' down there when ya don't have to.

GENNARO: *(Busted)* I knew I shouldn'ta married a smart girl.

DARLENE: So ya don't have to come home.

GENNARO: It's not so I don't have to come home.

(DARLENE sits. GENNARO stays very still, trying to gauge her response.)

GENNARO: Just another week and a half. That's all. I'll stop after New Year's.

EMMETT: *(Without looking at her)* Ya look okay.

LISA: *(Engrossed in the memo)* I am okay.

EMMETT: You sound…you don't sound like yourself.

LISA: No?

EMMETT: You're talking different.

LISA: I'm tryin' to get some of the Staten Island outta me.

EMMETT: What's wrong with sounding like where you're from?

LISA: This thing says that a hundred and twenty-three firefighters have been identified so far.

EMMETT: *(He turns to see what she's reading.)* Put that down. It's confidential.

LISA: Joey Kane is on here. October 6.

(EMMETT crosses to LISA and takes the memo out of her hands. He puts it back on the counter, face down.)

LISA: I had a crush on Joey when I was a kid.

EMMETT: I remember.

LISA: What does "tattoo" mean?

EMMETT: That's how we I D'd him.

(ANNIE *finishes her sandwich. She takes a bunch of cards out of her pocket and a pen. She starts sorting through them, making a "yes" pile and a "no" pile.* GENNARO *slowly sits.*)

LISA: So, is that all you're gonna eat? A piece and a half of toast?

EMMETT: For now.

LISA: I thought ya said you were hungry.

EMMETT: I was.

LISA: Lemme make ya somethin'.

EMMETT: I don't want anything else.

(EMMETT *puts the dirty dishes* LISA *moved back into the sink. She goes to the fridge and looks inside.*)

LISA: How come you don't got any groceries? Tell me ya eat more than toast. *(Checking out the cabinets.)* There are a few things in here. I'm sure I could come up with somethin'.

EMMETT: I don't have a taste for anything.

LISA: I could make ya—

EMMETT: *(Still with his back to her)* No.

(LISA *is staring into the cabinet. A pause. A gesture:*)

EMMETT: Do you want somethin'? Make yourself somethin'.

LISA: I don't eat breakfast.

(LISA *takes a small bottle of whisky out of the cabinet, looks at it briefly, puts it back. She's at a loss.*)

DARLENE: *(Quietly)* How long have you been lyin' about this.

GENNARO: I never lied.

DARLENE: Ya told me ya had to work.

GENNARO: I did have to work.

DARLENE: No, ya wanted to work.

GENNARO: Yeah, okay, I did. So we can have Christmas and still pay the goddamn bills.

DARLENE: *(Overlapping)* You'd rather work at Ground Zero—

GENNARO: *(Overlapping)* It's for the money. That's the reason. For the money.

DARLENE: *(Overlapping)* —than be here with us! Who cares about presents, Marco? There is no present you could buy me that I'd rather have then you bein' home.

GENNARO: Look, somethin' good has to come out of all this. For everybody down there. It ain't just me. We're all makin' a ton of overtime doin' this.

DARLENE: That is sick.

GENNARO: No, it's not. It is not fuckin' sick, Dar! Don't you think the guys who died would be doin' the same thing? If I was the one they were lookin' for, I'd want Jason or Billy or any of those guys to get whatever they could outta this. If it was me dead in that pile—

DARLENE: *(Overlapping)* Don't say that! I don't wanna hear you say that again—

GENNARO: *(Overlapping)* —I'd want them to get all the overtime they could. Somebody has to get somethin' outta this! Why not me? Why not us?

DARLENE: We already got somethin' outta this. You. Alive.

GENNARO: There's no way I woulda been down there that morning, even if I'd been workin'.

DARLENE: You don't know that. Look at Danny. He was there. Look what happened to him.

GENNARO: That's different.

DARLENE: It's not, Marco. It's just luck that you weren't Jason or Billy or even Danny. Luck. And now, you got this great gift, you're alive, you're okay, and what do you wanna do with the time ya been given? You wanna spend it in a graveyard. A toxic graveyard. So in ten years you can turn up with emphysema or cancer or god knows what, and *then* die. You are not just a cop and a "hero," Marco. You're my husband and Mikey's father, and your job is to come home to us every day.

(GENNARO *is surprised—this is the most emotional* DARLENE *has ever been about the matter. After a moment, he goes to her and hugs her.*)

GENNARO: Baby, baby, baby. Come on. Come on. I'm right here. I'm not gonna get sick. I'm not gonna die. Come on.

LISA: I guess I should go.

EMMETT: Ya gotta be somewhere?

LISA: Work.

EMMETT: What are ya doin' for work?

LISA: Nothin' interestin'.

EMMETT: Ya waitin' tables again?

LISA: No, thank god.

EMMETT: So? What kind of work?

LISA: It's boring.

EMMETT: All right. I won't ask any more questions.

(DARLENE *breaks the hug and exits.* GENNARO's *headache is killing him. He stands at the kitchen window and tries to get it together.*)

LISA: It's boring, that's all.

EMMETT: Yeah, okay, Lisa.

LISA: It is. I just answer phones for a rich guy in a stupid bankin' firm.

EMMETT: Where is this "stupid bankin' firm"?

LISA: Rockefeller Center.

EMMETT: Really? What floor?

LISA: Sixty-one.

EMMETT: *(Proudly)* Are you kiddin' me, Lisa? How's the view from up there?

LISA: Creepy. I'm a temp, Pop. It's nothin' to get excited about.

EMMETT: It's a job. That's always somethin' to get excited about.

LISA: Yeah. Well. It's excitin' til they blow up Rockefeller Center and you're pickin' pieces of *me* outta some pile.

EMMETT: That's not gonna happen.

LISA: It's a good target.

EMMETT: Not as good the Trade Center.

LISA: I worked there in July. I temped at Cantor Fitzgerald for two weeks.

(EMMETT and LISA are silent for a moment. GENNARO opens a few drawers, looking for a bottle of aspirin.)

EMMETT: What time ya gotta be at work?

LISA: I'm there nine to five. But today I told them I had a doctor's appointment.

EMMETT: How'd ya get here so early?

LISA: I stayed with Bobby and Janelle last night. He dropped me off here this morning on the way to some job. He's done with classes for the semester. You probably already know that.

EMMETT: I guess ya gotta get going. I don't want ya to screw up your job.

LISA: I hate my job. I don't really care if I screw it up.

EMMETT: Ya hate your paycheck, too?

LISA: It's just not what I wanted for my life.

EMMETT: Lisa, you're a kid. Stop talkin' like you're seventy. You can do whatever ya want.

LISA: I don't know what I want.

EMMETT: That's the thing. Ya gotta figure that out. Once ya do, you're all set.

LISA: *(She can't stand it another second.)* Dad, I have to ask you something.

EMMETT: Aw, here it comes.

LISA: What?

EMMETT: How much ya need? At least you're askin' instead of just takin'. That's somethin'.

LISA: Jesus. Forget this. Just fuckin' forget it.

EMMETT: Hey! Don't use language like that in my house!

LISA: It was real nice to see ya. Just like I remember it. Same old shit, different day.

(GENNARO fills a glass with water. LISA picks up her bag and goes to the closet to get her coat. She looks at his coat hanging on the inside of the door. She drops her bag and starts to check his pockets. He makes no effort to stop her. She takes a flask out of the inside pocket.)

EMMETT: Well, go on. Keep going if you're gonna go.

(LISA puts the flask on the kitchen table. She gets the whiskey bottle out of the cabinet and puts that on the table, too. GENNARO takes his aspirin. ANNIE unwraps the brownie.)

ANNIE: All right, gentlemen, are you ready for the best brownie in America? One taste of this and you will find instant nirvana. I'm serious—it's magic. Are you ready?

GENNARO: I thought it was the best brownie in the greater Metropolitan area.

ANNIE: It is. It's also the best brownie in America.

(ANNIE *cuts the brownie into three pieces. She takes her piece and waits for* EMMETT *and* GENNARO *to do the same. They are still in their own kitchens.* LISA *is looking at the alcohol.*)

ANNIE: Are you guys really going to make me eat this by myself?

(ANNIE *holds out their pieces of the brownie on napkins.* GENNARO *crosses, takes his, puts it on his tray, and sits. After a moment,* EMMETT *does the same.*)

ANNIE: You know, I don't think I've actually sat with a cop and a fireman at the same table before.

GENNARO: No surprise there.

ANNIE: Why is that?

GENNARO: Cops and firemen don't really hang out together.

ANNIE: But I would think in a situation like this—

GENNARO: In school, ya sat with your friends, right? Ya didn't sit with the people you didn't know.

ANNIE: Yes, but—

GENNARO: Why should this be any different?

EMMETT: (*Pointedly*) Because we're adults now.

(LISA *brings the whiskey bottle to the sink. She looks at* EMMETT.)

GENNARO: The truth is, Annie, cops and firemen don't really like each other.

EMMETT: That's not completely true.

ANNIE: Why don't cops and firemen like each other?

GENNARO: Well, I can tell ya why cops don't like firemen.

ANNIE: Actually, you know, we don't have to—

GENNARO: Firemen don't listen to anybody, they don't ever do what anybody tells 'em to do.

(LISA *uncaps the whiskey and pours it down the sink.*)

EMMETT: What he really means, Annie, is we don't listen to what cops tell us to do.

GENNARO: They always run right in and try to be heroes.

EMMETT: We're not trying to *be* anything. We're just doing our job.

GENNARO: This whole thing is a perfect example of that. They didn't listen to orders and they went in and stayed in when they shoulda got out—

EMMETT: *(Overlapping)* No one even heard the evacuation orders.

GENNARO: *(Overlapping)* —and then all hell broke loose, and now they're heroes.

ANNIE: I think we should change—

EMMETT: You wanna know why firemen don't like cops? Cops are arrogant.

GENNARO: Firemen are thieves. You should see what's in their trucks after they leave a fire.

EMMETT: Cops are corrupt and they lie.

GENNARO: I had a buddy who almost died on 9/11. He lost his partner that day. The department gave him time off and he took his family to Disney World. What did he see down there? A bunch of F D N Y who were takin' time off because they lost a gazillion guys from their firehouse. Were they there with their families? Nope. They ditched their wives and kids and went down there to have some fuckin' extended bachelor party—

EMMETT: We're all dealing with it differently—

(LISA *throws the empty bottle in the trash. She crosses to the flask, regards it for a moment, and then begins to search the cabinets.*)

ANNIE: Sorry. Sorry I asked. Let's change—

GENNARO: Fuckin' firemen are like goddamn New York City rock stars. Getting offered sex as they walk down the street in their gear on the way from the Pile to their cars. Fuckin' rock stars, but people still hate the cops. We died in that mess, too. We didn't lose 343, but we lost enough.

EMMETT: Rock stars?

GENNARO: You walk outta the hot zone, there are girls lined up practically throwin' themselves at ya, because a bunch of ya died. Our jobs are just as dangerous as yours, more, because we gotta deal with the public. You just gotta deal with buildings and houses that happen to be on fire.

EMMETT: Do ya have any idea what we do, ya idiot?

GENNARO: Did you just call me an idiot?

EMMETT: You sound like a jealous kid!

ANNIE: Guys! Stop it. Please.

(EMMETT *and* GENNARO *stop.* LISA *finishes with the cabinets and exits to search the rest of the house.*)

ANNIE: It seems to me that cops have a complicated job, politically. Tough decisions have to be made. Firemen save people's lives. The decisions they have to make aren't politically charged. Which is why it's easy to see firemen as heroes, and cops as…difficult.

EMMETT: That's a polite way to put it.

ANNIE: I see both jobs as equally dangerous, but one is more complex than the other.

GENNARO: You're exactly right, Annie. Being a cop is a lot harder than being a fireman.

ANNIE: That's not what I said.

EMMETT: I know what you meant.

GENNARO: Being a cop ain't no picnic.

EMMETT: Why do you do it if you don't like it?

GENNARO: Who said I didn't like it?

EMMETT: You just did.

GENNARO: I said it ain't no picnic. And there ain't no glory, that's for sure.

(ANNIE *leans forward to look at* GENNARO'*s nametag.*)

ANNIE: Gennaro? That's your last name.

GENNARO: Yeah. First name, Officer.

ANNIE: What's your real first name? The one your mother gave you.

GENNARO: Guess.

ANNIE: How am I going to guess? It could be anything. *(She looks at* EMMETT'*s shirt.)* Emmett?

EMMETT: Yup.

ANNIE: What's his name?

EMMETT: *(Squinting at his nametag)* Gennaro.

ANNIE: What's his first name?

(EMMETT *shrugs.* ANNIE *to* GENNARO:*)*

ANNIE: What's *his* first name?

(GENNARO *shrugs.*)

ANNIE: You guys don't know each other's names?

GENNARO: I know your name. Does that count?

ANNIE: You're arguing over the existence of God and you didn't introduce yourselves?

EMMETT: Jon.

ANNIE: And you?

GENNARO: Marco.

ANNIE: Jon Emmett and Marco Gennaro. Nice names.

GENNARO: You work with what you got, you know?

ANNIE: *(Laughing)* Yes, I do.

GENNARO: So, uh, Annie, when we goin' out?

EMMETT: Aw, come on. Leave her alone. That ain't why she's down here.

GENNARO: She's a big girl, she can handle it.

ANNIE: I'm very flattered, but I, um—

GENNARO: Can't blame a guy for tryin'.

EMMETT: Sometimes you can.

GENNARO: You got a boyfriend, don't ya.

EMMETT: And I think you got a wife and a kid.

GENNARO: She knows I'm just kiddin'.

EMMETT: How does she know that?

GENNARO: She just does. Right, Annie? So Annie, how's your boyfriend feel about you comin' down here?

ANNIE: You think you're the first person to ask me that in order to find out if I have a boyfriend?

GENNARO: You do, don't ya. You got a boyfriend.

ANNIE: I think I'm seeing someone.

GENNARO: Aw, you got a boyfriend.

ANNIE: No, no, no, it's not like that. I don't know what the situation is.

GENNARO: How long you been seeing him?

ANNIE: Not long.

GENNARO: Where'd ya meet him?

(ANNIE *doesn't say anything. Pause*)

GENNARO: Annie. You met him here, didn't you.

EMMETT: *(Teasing her)* Weren't you just tellin' us that stuff isn't supposed to happen down here?

GENNARO: I think I might have to confiscate your I D.

ANNIE: I knew I shouldn't have sat down here.

GENNARO: Is he a cop? He's a cop, isn't he.

EMMETT: Nah. I bet she don't like guns.

GENNARO: You don't have to like guns to go out with a cop. Come on, Annie, tell me, you datin' one of New York's Finest?

EMMETT: It ain't a cop.

GENNARO: Wanna bet?

EMMETT: Five bucks says it's a fireman.

GENNARO: Ten bucks says it's a cop.

EMMETT: Fine. Ten bucks.

(EMMETT *and* GENNARO *get out their wallets and slap their money down.*)

ANNIE: Put your money away. I'm going to get fired.

GENNARO: I still don't think they can fire you from a volunteer job.

EMMETT: Come on, Annie, money's on the table. Cop or fireman?

ANNIE: I'm not going to tell you.

(EMMETT *and* GENNARO *just sit there, staring* ANNIE *down.*)

ANNIE: This is crazy. Come on.

(EMMETT *and* GENNARO *won't budge. She sighs.*)

ANNIE: Fireman.

(EMMETT *cheers,* GENNARO *groans. All three speak at once.*)

GENNARO: *(Simultaneously)* Sonofabitch! Aw, Annie, what're you doin' with a fireman? Didn't you learn nothin' from being down here?

ANNIE: *(Simultaneously)* SSSSSSHHHHHH! Don't yell! Be quiet! You're going to get me in trouble! SSSSSSHHHHHHH!

EMMETT: *(Simultaneously)* I knew it. I knew it. Good choice, Annie, good choice. I hope you didn't give him your number in the tent, Annie, we'll have to turn you in to the shift supervisor. What's his name? I bet I know him.

ANNIE: How could you know him? There are twelve thousand firemen in New York City. You don't know him.

EMMETT: So you can tell me his name. You got nothin' to worry about.

(EMMETT *reaches for the money.* GENNARO *puts his hand on it to stop him. To* ANNIE*:*)

GENNARO: Just a fireman, Annie? Tell me he's at least a lieutenant.

ANNIE: I'm not telling either of you anything else. I've told you enough.

GENNARO: *(To* EMMETT*)* Lieutenant.

EMMETT: Naw. She's not old enough. She wouldn't go out with an officer. Look at her. She's just a kid.

*(*ANNIE *looks at* EMMETT *skeptically.)*

GENNARO: Lieutenant or captain, it's mine.

EMMETT: Fine.

*(*ANNIE *says nothing.* EMMETT *and* GENNARO *stare. Finally she relents.)*

ANNIE: Captain.

*(*GENNARO *whoops and snatches the money off the table.* EMMETT *looks concerned.)*

EMMETT: A captain? How old's the guy? He's not married, is he?

ANNIE: Divorced.

EMMETT: Kids?

ANNIE: Four boys.

GENNARO: Jesus.

EMMETT: All right, you came this far, you might as well give me the rest.

GENNARO: *(Admiring his winnings)* Be careful, Annie, Emmett here's a captain, too. He probably knows him. All those guys know each other.

EMMETT: I gotta tell ya, Annie, any guy worth his salt doesn't walk out on his family.

GENNARO: Aw, come on, don't scare her like that. You don't know nothin' about the guy.

EMMETT: I know he left his family and he's dating 20-year-olds.

ANNIE: Okay, for the record, you're off by a few years.

GENNARO: How off?

ANNIE: Off. Let's leave it at that.

EMMETT: If ya tell me his name, I can tell ya if you're in trouble or not. You know, some guys are good guys, some ain't, even in the fire department.

GENNARO: "Even in the fire department." Come on.

EMMETT: I'm just saying, I can tell her if she should stick around or not.

GENNARO: *(He thinks about this for a second.)* He's got a point, Annie. It can't hurt to get a second opinion, right?

ANNIE: You'll keep this to yourself? Both of you?

GENNARO: *(Simultaneously)* Who am I gonna tell?

EMMETT: *(Simultaneously)* Of course, yeah.

ANNIE: Billy Allen.

GENNARO: *(To* EMMETT:*)* Do you know him?

EMMETT: Yeah.

GENNARO: Well?

EMMETT: The truth?

GENNARO: No, she wants you to lie to her. Yeah, the truth.

ANNIE: Please don't tell me he's not really divorced.

EMMETT: In the firehouse, we'd say…aw, never mind that. Just stay away from the guy.

ANNIE: Why? What were you going to say?

EMMETT: He gets around, that's all. He has a… reputation.

ANNIE: *That's* what you say in the firehouse?

EMMETT: We have an expression for guys like him. You don't need to hear it.

ANNIE: Oh, come on. You can't do that to me. What were you going to say?

EMMETT: *(Sighs)* That guy gets more ass than a toilet seat.

GENNARO: Wow. I never heard that one before. *(Laughing)* That's a new one on me.

(GENNARO stops laughing when ANNIE puts her head in her hands. Awkward silence)

EMMETT: You okay? You're not…crying, are you?

GENNARO: Aw, Jesus, ya made her cry.

(EMMETT tentatively reaches out to touch her arm.)

EMMETT: Sorry. I just thought ya should know. Ya know?

GENNARO: Nice goin'.

ANNIE: *(She looks up, dry-eyed.)* It's fine. I'm fine.

EMMETT: Listen. There are hundreds of other guys down here who'd love to take you out.

GENNARO: Correct me if I'm wrong here, Annie, *(To* EMMETT:*)* but I don't think that's the point.

ANNIE: I've always been a sucker for the bad ones.

GENNARO: *(Shaking his head:)* That's what you get for goin' out with a fireman. Those guys'll get ya every time.

ANNIE: Blinded by the bunker gear.

EMMETT: You wouldn't be the first. I'm sorry, Annie.

ANNIE: Hey, at least you won ten bucks, Officer.

GENNARO: Yeah. Maybe you should have it.

ANNIE: No, no, no. You won it. You keep it.

EMMETT: He don't deserve ya, Annie.

GENNARO: No, he don't.

ANNIE: *(She smiles, embarrassed. She starts working on her card pile again)* Thanks.

(DARLENE enters. She's dressed. She drops an overnight bag on the counter. GENNARO turns around. He watches as she packs Mikey's sippy cups and special plate.)

GENNARO: *(To DARLENE)* Whaddya doin'?

DARLENE: Mikey and I aren't gonna be here when you get home.

GENNARO: You threaten me with that every other day.

DARLENE: This time I mean it.

GENNARO: You say that every other day, too.

(DARLENE keeps packing and doesn't respond. GENNARO wearily crosses to her in the kitchen.)

GENNARO: Dar, come on. Just a few more days. Trust me. It's gonna be worth it.

DARLENE: It's money, Marco. It's fucking money.

GENNARO: Aw, not the F word. You know I hate that.

DARLENE: Fucking money.

GENNARO: You are so fuckin' stubborn, ya know that?

DARLENE: Oh, it's okay for you to swear at me?

GENNARO: Jesus Christ.

DARLENE: Stop takin' the Lord's name in vain.

GENNARO: Stop sayin' that to me.

DARLENE: Stop doin' it.

GENNARO: God, you drive me fuckin' crazy.

DARLENE: Well then I guess it's a good thing I won't be here when you get home tonight.

GENNARO: It's *tomorrow*. I'll be home *tomorrow*. You got a selective memory problem.

DARLENE: I don't give a shit *when* you're coming home, you lyin' son of a bitch!

(DARLENE *picks up a pot and hurls it at him. It hits the wall and leaves an ugly mark and a dent. *GENNARO *starts to laugh. She doesn't. He can't stop, which pisses her off more. They inspect the dent together. There is a series of dents that have been repaired to some degree.)*

GENNARO: That's a deep one, Dar.

DARLENE: What? You can fix that. Ya do it all the time.

GENNARO: Usually you throw a plate or a glass, and it breaks when it hits the wall, so it doesn't do much damage.

DARLENE: You've fixed worse than that.

GENNARO: I don't know, Dar, this one's pretty bad. We might have to get Sal in here.

DARLENE: We're not callin' the stinkin' landlord. It's not that bad. It's not. Look at it compared to this one. This one was a lot deeper.

GENNARO: What's that one from?

DARLENE: The time you wanted to go on a golf trip with the boys a week after Mikey was born.

GENNARO: Oh yeah. What's this one?

DARLENE: The time you forgot to tell me about your nephew's christening.

GENNARO: I still don't get why ya were so mad about that.

DARLENE: And knowing you, ya never will.

GENNARO: This new one's pretty bad.

DARLENE: Oh, so what, Marco. What do we care? We still rent the damn place.

(GENNARO *smiles.)*

DARLENE: What now. What. You think this is funny? What.

GENNARO: Nothin'.

DARLENE: Nothin'. Right. Of course. I don't even know why I bother to ask. My soon-to-be ex-husband, the Mystery Man.

GENNARO: I'm goin'. I'll call ya later.

DARLENE: I already told ya. I won't be here.

GENNARO: Then I'll call ya on your cell.

DARLENE: Don't bother, Marco. I'm done.

(DARLENE *exits with her bags.* LISA *comes back into the kitchen empty-handed and picks up the flask.*)

GENNARO: "Have a good day, honey." "Thanks, Dar. You, too." Dar? Hey, Dar?

(GENNARO *waits for a response.* LISA *uncaps the flask and smells the contents.*)

LISA: Pop. You could lose your job.

EMMETT: It ain't your problem, Lisa.

LISA: Yeah, it is.

EMMETT: Are ya still doin' the drugs?

LISA: What do you think?

EMMETT: I think that's my answer.

LISA: Then I guess it doesn't matter what I say, does it. I'm not, but I'm sure ya don't believe me.

EMMETT: If you're not, why couldn't ya just answer me straight.

LISA: I wanted to know what you'd say.

EMMETT: You're all grown up. You can do what ya want.

LISA: Yeah, well, so can you.

EMMETT: Yeah, thanks.

LISA: So when did ya start again?

EMMETT: Why?

LISA: It's too bad, that's all. You were sober for a long time. I always admired that. I thought about it a lot in rehab.

(EMMETT *turns to look at her, surprised. He didn't know about rehab.*)

LISA: Mom would be upset if she knew.

EMMETT: Oh, she knows. She definitely knows. Your mother can see everythin' from up there.

LISA: You a believer again?

(GENNARO *gives up and comes back to the table.*)

EMMETT: Whoever said I wasn't?

LISA: Bobby.

EMMETT: I didn't know you and Bobby talked so much.

LISA: He told me ya stopped going to church with them.

EMMETT: I stopped for a while after you left.

LISA: I didn't leave, Pop. You threw me out.

EMMETT: I stopped for a while after I threw you out. But I started goin' again. A different place.

LISA: When?

EMMETT: About a year and a half after she died.

LISA: That's, like, a year ago.

EMMETT: Uh huh.

LISA: Just in time.

EMMETT: For what?

LISA: All this. I'm glad. I'm glad you been goin', that's all.

(EMMETT *crosses into the kitchen. He takes the flask from* LISA's *hands and puts it back on the counter.*)

LISA: I wanna come back, Dad.

EMMETT: I'm lettin' ya keep that key, ain't I?

LISA: I'm talkin' about movin' home. To help out.

EMMETT: Whaddya wanna come home for? You were just telling me how great Manhattan is.

LISA: I wanna come home because I think it would be good.

EMMETT: What the hell are ya talkin' about?

LISA: I think it would be good. For me. And for you.

EMMETT: I'm not stupid, Lisa.

LISA: You're never gonna forgive me.

EMMETT: I try. Believe me. I try real hard. But it ain't easy. You took a lot of money from me.

LISA: It was two years ago, Dad. I'm a different person now.

EMMETT: How different can you be?

LISA: I went to rehab. I have a job. I support myself. I'm savin' to pay you back every single cent. I don't do drugs or drink anymore. Which is more than I can say for you.

EMMETT: That's not your business.

LISA: I wanna make it my business.

EMMETT: The blind leading the blind, huh?

LISA: She asked me to take care of you.

EMMETT: *(He processes this information.)* When?

LISA: I don't know. One day. We were just sittin' around, and I was gettin' on her case about those stupid cigarettes. She said, "If I die, honey, you gotta take care of Dad. 'Cause lord knows he can't do it himself, and Bobby and Jimmy wouldn't know how."

EMMETT: Yeah, well, I'm your father, and it's in my contract to take care of you, so I guess we both failed.

LISA: How did we fail? We haven't even tried.

EMMETT: Maybe you haven't.

LISA: You just...you didn't know what to do. And I didn't either. I chose wrong.

EMMETT: Who got ya hooked?

LISA: *(This is an old conversation.)* Oh, Dad. I did. I did it myself.

EMMETT: But who gave ya the drugs?

LISA: This is New York. Anyone can get anythin', anytime, anywhere.

EMMETT: So who was it?

LISA: There was nothin' ya could have done.

EMMETT: Depends. Who was it?

LISA: When did ya start drinking again?

EMMETT: What kind of an answer is that?

LISA: You want to know somethin', I want to know somethin'. I'll tell you if you tell me.

EMMETT: I'm your father. It doesn't work that way.

LISA: You been wantin' me to answer that question for a long time.

EMMETT: *(A stand-off. He relents.)* You first.

LISA: At the same time.

EMMETT: What is this, grade school?

LISA: Yeah. That's exactly what it is. Grade school. Ready?

EMMETT: Aw, come on. This is stupid.

LISA: Yeah, sure, whatever. Ready? One, two, three.

(Neither EMMETT nor LISA says anything.)

LISA: Wow. How about that. I guess ya could say we have some trust issues, huh?

(EMMETT tries to hide the fact that he finds this funny. LISA is pleased that she made him smile.)

LISA: Okay, come on. Let's just get it over with. Come on, come on, come on. Ready? One, two, three.

EMMETT: *(Simultaneously)* The 12th.

LISA: *(Simultaneously)* Dominic.

EMMETT: I knew it. I always knew it.

LISA: He didn't make me do anything I didn't wanna do.

EMMETT: That's the worst part about havin' a daughter, ya know that? Just wait. Wait until you got your own kid and she's goin' out with some no-good loser and you know what he's doin' to her when you're not around but there's not a damn thing you can do about it. Just wait. It kills ya. It keeps ya up at night. It's enough to drive ya crazy.

LISA: September 12th, huh?

EMMETT: *(He shrugs.)* After twenty-one hours on the Pile, we went for a drink.

LISA: I read that, like, half the alcoholics working down there fell off the wagon at some point in the last three months.

EMMETT: That's all?

LISA: Ya talked to anyone about it?

EMMETT: Like who?

LISA: Anyone.

EMMETT: Father McManus.

LISA: What does he say?

EMMETT: He says I'm excused from apologizing for my sins for the next few months.

LISA: That's convenient.

EMMETT: I thought so.

LISA: Talk to any counselors?

EMMETT: What for?

LISA: Well, let's see. For starters, the fact that a hundred of your friends died. That might give ya a good reason to talk to 'em. Add on top of that the fact that ya were sober for a million years and now you're not. They might be interested in that, too.

EMMETT: I don't wanna talk to those people.

LISA: Whaddya mean, "those people"? They're there for you. To help you. The city of New York is paying for you to have counseling available, like, twenty-four hours a day right now. You know this city—it's cheap and stingy. It won't pay for anything unless it's necessary. So "those people" must be necessary.

EMMETT: I don't need to talk to 'em.

LISA: Do ya wanna stop drinkin', Dad?

EMMETT: *(Definitively:)* Not right now I don't, Miss Ten-Step Program.

LISA: It's twelve steps.

EMMETT: Whatever.

LISA: You never did the steps?

EMMETT: I didn't have to. I had your mother.

LISA: How was Mom a substitute for A A?

EMMETT: She told me if I didn't stop drinkin', she wouldn't marry me. And when I stopped, she told me if I started again, she wouldn't give me any kids. And that if I started again when we had kids, she'd take them and leave. It was all pretty clear.

LISA: I never heard that story before.

EMMETT: Yeah, well, it's not exactly somethin' ya tell your children.

LISA: Was it hard to stop?

EMMETT: Nope. I wanted to marry your mother more than I'd ever wanted anything.

LISA: And you were sober all that time?

EMMETT: Almost. *(Pause)* I took a few sips at one point.

LISA: When?

EMMETT: After you were born.

LISA: Why?

EMMETT: I don't know. It was just one night. I never did it again. I had no idea what to do with a baby. You were loud.

LISA: Did Mom find out?

EMMETT: *(He nods.)* I told her.

LISA: What did she say?

EMMETT: That's between me and your mother.

LISA: What about A A, Dad?

EMMETT: It's not the time for me to start somethin' like that.

LISA: I'm worried about ya livin' here alone right now.

EMMETT: I been livin' here alone for a few years. I think I'm doin' fine, all things considered.

LISA: You could use some help with the dishes. So what if I came home?

(EMMETT *regards* LISA *carefully for a moment.*)

EMMETT: Why would I want you home with me right now, Lisa? You're the only person who didn't call. Every teacher I ever had called me. Everyone from the neighborhood came by. People I went to school with who moved away called me. Every guy I ever worked with. Your mother's whole family. Janelle's whole family. Bobby's old girlfriends. Jimmy's old girlfriends. Their mothers. Even the Millers, he's stationed in Germany now, they called me. My phone rang nonstop for a week. Jimmy finally changed the message on the machine: "Dad's here, he's fine. He'll call you back in a few months. Thanks for your message." I heard voices from thirty years ago on that thing. But not yours.

LISA: The last time I saw you, you were throwin' me out of the house. You wouldn't even let me come in to get my stuff.

EMMETT: I had every right to do that.

LISA: No, you didn't. I needed help.

EMMETT: Ya gave up your right to help from me.

LISA: I needed help before I took your money. You just didn't notice. You couldn't even look at us after Mom left.

EMMETT: She didn't leave. She died.

LISA: It's the same thing, Dad. (*She looks away from him.*)

EMMETT: No, it's not. It's not the same thing. Lisa, look at me.

(LISA *doesn't.*)

EMMETT: Sweetheart.

(LISA *looks at* EMMETT, *surprised by his tenderness.*)

EMMETT: It's not the same thing.

(EMMETT and LISA are silent for a while.)

LISA: I was tempin' at N Y U that day, and I was walking through Washington Square Park. And the first thought that went through my head was, Dad's gonna go up there and try to save those people. And I stood in the same spot for the next hour and a half, lookin' at the Towers above that arch, until they were both gone. And then I thought, that's it, he's dead, and I never fixed things. If I'd still been tempin' there, maybe I woulda died instead of him. I thought, I deserved that, not Dad.

EMMETT: Lisa—

LISA: I called Bobby—I don't know why my phone was workin'. He told me you were on duty but he couldn't get through on your cell. He said, "Go home and wait. I'll call you when I know somethin'." When he called and said that you had checked in, I didn't believe him. I was sure that they made a mistake, and that you were down there, somewhere, crushed, or in pieces. I was afraid to call 'cause I didn't think you'd answer. A few days later, I finally got the guts, and I called. I called ya a million times. And every time I got that damn answerin' machine, I was more and more afraid.

EMMETT: Jimmy changed the message.

LISA: That made it worse 'cause it wasn't your voice anymore. It was like ya didn't live there, like when ya changed the message after mom died. I thought, God, now they're both gone. Bobby and Jimmy kept askin' me if I'd seen ya, so then I thought, well, I'll just go over there. I'll just show up, and I'll wait until he's there. But I hadn't hit my one year mark yet, and I thought, if he doesn't show up, I don't know what I'll do. I might do somethin' I shouldn't. And I wanted to hit that mark. So I promised myself I wouldn't come lookin' for ya unless I hit it.

EMMETT: When is it?

LISA: Today, Pop.

EMMETT: Well. That's somethin'.

LISA: It's somethin'.

EMMETT: Your mother would be proud of ya.

LISA: No, she wouldn't. She'd be mad at me.

EMMETT: For what?

LISA: For everything.

EMMETT: Your mother's a forgivin' woman. How do ya think she stayed married to me for twenty-six years? If she's mad at anybody, she's mad at me. She woulda done things different. *(He stands.)* Nothin' ya did could make ya deserve to die, Lisa. Nothin'.

(LISA nods, almost embarrassed by her confessions.)

EMMETT: I been up all night. I gotta sleep.

LISA: I'll call in today and stay here. I could buy some groceries while you're sleeping. Then we could have lunch. Or dinner.

EMMETT: No. Thanks, though.

LISA: Well, what do ya think about me movin' back in here with ya?

EMMETT: I know ya want an answer, but I don't have one. So go to work.

LISA: When will ya have an answer?

EMMETT: I gotta finish this thing. I'm not doin' anythin' until it's all over.

LISA: What about Christmas?

EMMETT: What about it?

LISA: Can I see ya on Christmas?

EMMETT: I gotta work. I'm not really up for celebratin' the birth of the lord anyway.

LISA: I thought ya said you were back at church.

EMMETT: I am. I made my peace with everythin'. But I'm gonna sit this one out this year.

LISA: What about New Year's?

EMMETT: Gotta work.

LISA: Both holidays? That's not fair. Can't ya get someone to cover ya?

(EMMETT *shrugs*.)

LISA: Dad, just let me…I don't think ya should—

EMMETT: That's enough, Lisa. Go on.

(LISA *doesn't move*.)

EMMETT: I can't decide what to eat half the time. The reason I don't got any groceries is 'cause I go to the store and I stand there, lookin' at the rows and rows of food and I can't pick anything. I don't even remember what I like. So don't ask me to make any decisions.

LISA: You gotta eat.

EMMETT: You're just like your mother, ya know that?

LISA: You haven't said that to me in a long time.

EMMETT: I haven't seen ya in a long time.

LISA: I don't know what I woulda done, Dad.

(LISA *walks to* EMMETT *and kisses him on the cheek. She gets her bag and coat, and leaves. He looks at the flask on the counter.* GENNARO's *attention is caught by something downstage*.)

GENNARO: Shit. Look at that.

(EMMETT *looks*.)

GENNARO: What's he still doin' here?

EMMETT: He's shakin' hands.

ANNIE: Who is that?

GENNARO: Robertson.

ANNIE: Chief Robertson?

(EMMETT comes back to the table but doesn't sit.)

GENNARO: Yeah. He found his son today. He was a cop.

EMMETT: Found his other son in October. Fireman.

GENNARO: The guy ain't slept since September.

EMMETT: Some guys think he should keep lookin' for everybody else's sons, but I say, after losing two, he can go home.

GENNARO: And do what? Get back to his retirement and play golf every day?

EMMETT: Get back to his family.

GENNARO: What family? He probably wishes he'd never brought those two boys into this world.

EMMETT: I bet he thinks those kids are the best thing he ever did.

(A pause)

GENNARO: It sure is fucked up. *(To ANNIE)* Excuse me.

ANNIE: *(As in, "Don't worry about it.")* It's fine.

(They watch Robertson shake hands. When he leaves, Emmett sits. Annie looks at the two men who are lost in thought.)

ANNIE: Can I get you guys anything else to eat or drink?

(GENNARO shakes his head.)

EMMETT: No, thanks.

ANNIE: Well. The tables are a mess, I have cards to hand out, and I think I'm about to get scolded for fraternizing. So. It was really nice to meet you both. *(She gathers up the cards.)*

EMMETT: Oh yeah, we're a barrel of laughs today.

ANNIE: I always enjoy a spirited discussion.

(EMMETT chuckles.)

ANNIE: You guys need anything from the back? We just got in boots, socks, insoles, gloves—

EMMETT/GENNARO: *(Ad lib)* No, I'm good. / I've got plenty of that stuff already. / Thanks, though.

ANNIE: Okay. Don't forget to eat your brownie. *(She takes a card out of her back pocket.)* Here. The kids in my class made this. It's safe—I checked.

(ANNIE tries to hand it to GENNARO.)

GENNARO: No, thanks. I had enough of those for one day.

EMMETT: I'll take it.

ANNIE: I'm almost afraid to leave you two here without a mediator. Flag me down if you're going to have any more discussions about religion. I'll see you later. *(She exits.)*

EMMETT: Would it have killed ya to take the card?

GENNARO: Like I said, I had enough of Jesus for one day.

EMMETT: There is such a thing as being polite, ya know.

GENNARO: You're the one who said her boyfriend "gets more ass than a toilet seat." You really laid it on the line for her about that guy.

EMMETT: I did her a favor. She don't need to saddle herself with some divorced guy.

GENNARO: Guys get divorced for all kinds of reasons, ya know.

EMMETT: Usually it's the wrong ones.

GENNARO: You said you ain't got somebody waiting for you at home. So where's your wife?

EMMETT: Why?

GENNARO: You're so busy talkin' about how divorced guys are slime, I wonder where your wife is, that's all. Never been married?

EMMETT: I been married.

GENNARO: So you're divorced.

EMMETT: I ain't divorced.

GENNARO: So where's your wife? *(He realizes.)* Sorry.

(After an awkward silence, EMMETT *makes a peace offering.)*

EMMETT: Finish your Christmas shoppin' yet?

GENNARO: No. But I know what I'm gettin'.

EMMETT: You got any good ideas for me?

GENNARO: I only got one good idea, and if you already own your house, it won't do you any good.

EMMETT: Oh yeah? You buyin' your house?

GENNARO: This next paycheck should give me the rest of my down payment.

EMMETT: Congratulations.

GENNARO: I been keepin' it a secret but the wife is gonna divorce me 'cause of all the fuckin' hours I'm workin'. I ain't gonna blow it now, though. Not after bustin' my ass down here for three months.

EMMETT: Well, you're getting' somethin' good outta all this.

GENNARO: Yeah, well, we'll see. There's a good chance I'll be spending Christmas alone this year.

EMMETT: I ain't even thought about what I'm gettin' people.

GENNARO: That's gonna get ya in trouble.

EMMETT: Can't get my mind on it. You said you got kids?

GENNARO: Mikey.

EMMETT: That's it?

GENNARO: The wife wants a whole house full of 'em, but the world's too crazy. One's enough.

EMMETT: Some women were made to be mothers, ya know. *(Indicating* ANNIE *as he opens the card she gave him.)* Like that girl. That's the kind of girl ya marry and ya give her as many kids as she wants.

GENNARO: I could be wrong, but it sounds like you got a little crush there, Captain.

EMMETT: I'm not the one who asked her out.

*(*GENNARO *laughs a little.)*

EMMETT: She just reminds me of someone, that's all.

*(*EMMETT *pushes his tray away and reads the card from* ANNIE.*)*

GENNARO: *(Indicating the sandwich)* Aren't you gonna eat that thing?

*(*EMMETT *shakes his head, distracted, reading.)*

GENNARO: You gotta be kidding me. After all that, you're not gonna eat it? *(He looks closely at the sandwich.)* It's practically a freakin' work of art or something. You could bronze the damn thing.

*(*EMMETT *finishes, then hands him the card.)*

GENNARO: No.

EMMETT: Don't worry, Jesus ain't in there anywhere.

GENNARO: Aw, come on.

EMMETT: She wanted you to have it, the least you can do is read it. Go on. It won't bite ya.

(GENNARO *reluctantly takes the card and reads aloud.*)

GENNARO: "Dear Firemen and Firewomen and Policemen and Policewomen and E S U police and F B I Agents and A T F Agents and Construction Workers and Steel Workers and Machinery Drivers and E M Ts and Security Workers and Volunteers and anybody I accidentally forget—I hope you are okay. It's hard what you have to do. Sometimes things are hard. But then sometimes things get better. I hope you find all your friends. Don't worry—they know you are doing everything you can."

(GENNARO *hands the card back to* EMMETT, *who puts it in his pocket.* EMMETT *takes one bite of his brownie and reads the Times.* GENNARO's *head hurts. He checks his cell phone. No messages. Lights out*)

END OF PLAY

www.ingramcontent.com/pod-product-compliance
Lightning Source LLC
Chambersburg PA
CBHW052208090426
42741CB00010B/2454